BECOMING A MISSIONARY

Missionaries who represent the Church of Jesus Christ of Latter-day Saints are considered representatives of not only the church but of Jesus Christ. Their purpose is inviting and teaching others to come to Jesus Christ. They are between the ages of 18 and 26 and spend a total of two years for men and 18 months for women dedicating all of their time to this purpose. The schedule is very strict during that time allowing only for about one hour a week for emailing family and only two times a year they get to call home. They have no television, video games, radios or other devices that might distract them from their calling. Naturally in order to be able to take on such an important and selfless role, these men and women spend years in preparation for the task. Just like every other calling in the church there is no compensation for missionary service which means preparing to serve also involves saving money and/or having sponsors who help pay.

You might ask: why would young men and women want to take on such a task? The reason for this is that they believe that after the death of the Apostles, Christ's church was taken away from the world. After many years when the world was finally ready, Our Heavenly Father and His son

Jared Ray Hunt

Jesus Christ appeared to Joseph Smith in the spring of 1820 and called him to be the prophet that would restore their church and bring back the proper authority for saving ordinances like baptism and eternal marriage.

Serving as a missionary for the Church of Jesus Christ of Latter-Day Saints was a goal I always had since I was a little child. I had a friend in my youth who was about my age but more mature than me. He had a great desire to "serve a mission". At church he would often request for us to sing songs about missionary work and he glowed with enthusiasm. Before meeting him, becoming a missionary was just something I knew was asked of us. I hadn't really thought about it in great detail before, but he helped me see that it was something I should work for and look forward to. As I followed his example at a young age I soon started to make changes in my life to become worthy of missionary service.

When I was 12 years old he died in a four-wheeler accident. At his funeral I joined a group of young men to sing one of his favorite church songs which was about missionary work. It was at that time I once again reevaluated my life and became even more motivated to serve. I wanted to honor his example and be the missionary he always wanted us both to be someday. Every choice I made from then on was with the lingering thought of how it could affect my ability to serve a mission. Whenever I was on the edge of doing anything out of line I stayed within the boundaries of what I knew wouldn't find me unworthy or unable to serve.

At age 16 when my oldest brother returned from missionary service in Brazil, I was able to spend time with him in Nauvoo, Illinois which is where Joseph Smith and early members of the church were last settled before he was wrongfully imprisoned in a nearby town called Carthage and murdered along with his brother Hyrum. Being there I took advantage of the history and spent time reflecting and praying. I eventually received a strong spiritual feeling that he was actually called by God to be a prophet and restore His church. I had felt impressions before in my life but this one came with such clarity, I could never deny it.

Unfortunately, when I returned home after this great experience, I made several bad choices. While in Nauvoo, I had lost a considerable amount of weight and was very borderline unhealthy. This led to my decision to not play football in school that year which meant I had a lot more time on my hands. As idle hands are the devil's playground it was not soon after that I developed an unhealthy addiction that I would struggle with for many years to come.

Becoming a missionary for the Church of Jesus Christ of Latter-day Saints takes a lot more than simply packing up and going. One needs to be physically, mentally, emotionally, and spiritually prepared. In my experience the biggest struggle usually is being spiritually worthy to serve. Being worthy requires a commitment to living the commandments set by both prophets of old and modern-day prophets who have led the church since it's restoration. These commandments begin with the original 10 given to Moses and continue with several others. Some more noteworthy of these are abstinence from premarital intercourse and addictive substances like coffee, tea, and alcohol.

By the time I turned 19 -which at the time was the

age most young men served missions- I was still struggling with addiction and seen as unworthy for missionary service. It was not an addiction severely heinous as to automatically disqualify me from ever serving, but it was significant enough to require a good amount of abstinence and recovery before being able to serve. During those dark years I never completely forgot my previous commitment to my religion and my friend or the feelings I often had that it was very important to serve. It was just hard to fight the addiction. After about two years of wandering around in the dark, with the help of family, friends, and church leaders I finally was able to abstain from my addiction long enough to be found as a worthy member again.

I soon started working on my missionary papers and at about the same time my older sister decided to turn in her papers as well. After a couple of interviews and getting everything from finances to dental work in order I finally sent in my paperwork to the church headquarters. When the paperwork arrives leaders of the church read through it and prays for inspiration. Based on this inspiration they determine to which part of the world each missionary should go. Within about a month, my sister and I received letters on the same day. My letter stated that I was called to serve in Argentina and that I would be spending the first two months of my two-year term in the Missionary Training Center (MTC) in Provo, Utah before heading to my final destination. My sister was assigned to serve in Florida and was set to report to the MTC about a month before I was as I needed more time to get a passport and paperwork together for a visa.

When my sister left for the MTC we were all happy for her and she shined with excitement. After about five weeks there, she became very ill and was sent back home. She was released from missionary service and was eventually told she could never return as her health did not permit it. To this day she still fights the same illness though it has unfortunately progressed. While she was at the MTC she was an inspiration to many other missionaries and even had an opportunity to teach someone on the plane ride home about our beliefs. In no way did we ever think that her time there was wasted or that she failed or even that going there in the first place wasn't inspired. Though she did not serve for the full 18-month term, she still served a successful mission in her time.

Once a member receives their letter from the church about their missionary assignment, they still get a choice whether or not to accept the calling. They are given the task right away to write a letter back that states their decision. I'm sure it is rare that at that point anyone would reject the assignment since there is a lot one has to do before even getting the letter, but in the church, there is nothing left to be assumed when it comes to callings. When the prospective missionary writes their letter of confirmation they are fully committed to serving the full term being 18 months for women and two years for men. The only way that a mission term is honorably shortened is because of medical problems. My sister accepted her calling at the time knowing she was healthy enough for the task and being completely committed to serving the full 18 months. She was rightfully devastated to return early but soon accepted the experience for the learning experience that it was.

After she came back I had about two weeks to prepare before reporting.

MISSIONARY LIFE

When I finally arrived at to the MTC, I felt like I had already accomplished one of the greatest goals in my life. From the moment I stepped on the grounds, I made a commitment to do everything the right way. After all, I had worked hard and made several life changes to just get to this point and I wasn't going to waste any time in my two-year term by being disobedient to the rules and regulations set for missionaries by the church. I made it my goal to be the best possible missionary I could be. I was there with a purpose and I had so many people to honor with my service, especially my sister and my childhood friend.

The MTC can be a very stressful experience as it is an adjustment period to the missionary schedule and way of life. At first, we were assigned colleagues that in the church we refer to as companions. In most cases a companionship is just two missionaries but at times there are three. During the time of this companionship both missionaries are responsible for each other. They go everywhere together. They share the same room in whatever living situation they're in. A missionary is never alone. The only exception is when a they are in an interview or in the bathroom at which point their companion is waiting nearby. It is not completely uncommon for companions to have problems getting along as they are together all the time until assigned to be with someone else. In the MTC I was assigned

Dear God,

the same companion during the whole two months there which is normal. When out in the field every 6 weeks there are transfers where if assignments change, they will usually take place then. I was lucky to have a very understanding and easy-going companion in the MTC. He was as determined as I was to be obedient and work hard. We pushed each other to be our best. Though we both struggled to learn Spanish, by the time we left the MTC we felt confident enough to contribute to lessons and get around. Soon we finally received our travel plans and boarded planes.

After about a 14-hour flight to Argentina we then took another plane to my specific area. When we boarded the plane, I sat between two men who only spoke Spanish. While we waited to take off, the flight attendants began passing out boxes. I had no idea what was inside them and as I looked around I saw other missionaries ahead of me reject them. I had thought that maybe there was food inside, but the boxes were closed. I also didn't have any foreign money yet on me and didn't know if they would cost anything. As I saw the other missionaries reject them I thought that surely, they were as hungry as I was for I had hardly eaten much in the last 14 hours. When the attendants approached my row, I didn't want to embarrass myself by asking anything so like others before me I rejected the box. After they moved on, I was devastated to see the man next to me open the box and pull out a sandwich and drink.

I have often reflected on that experience and especially more so during my time as a missionary. I knew that like those boxes the message I had to teach those around me was something very desirable and that would spiritually feed them. I also knew that if I didn't work hard to be able to teach in a way that they could understand, then they really wouldn't be able to know if they wanted to accept or reject what I had to offer. If anyone had explained to me what was in the boxes and if they cost anything, then I would've been able to make a better-informed decision. I resolved to be as transparent as possible whenever I taught.

Once we finally made it to my assigned area, we met our mission president. After meeting with each of us newcomers he assigned us companions that would be our trainers. For at least the next 6 weeks we would be together with these missionaries as they show us the ropes and how to apply the things we learned in the MTC to the field. My trainer was very relaxed and for the most part we got a long pretty well. He helped me further understand the importance of strictly following the mission schedule every day.

The mission daily schedule in the field is very similar to this:

- **6:30 a.m.** Wake up, pray, exercise, and do other preparations for the day.
- **7:30 a.m.** Breakfast.
- **8:00 a.m.** Personal study.
- **9:00 a.m.** Companion study.
- **10:00 a.m.** Language study for 30min.
- **10:30 a.m.** Begin daily plans going to teaching appointments and finding people to teach.
- **Lunch:** One hour if possible, with members and then back to teaching appointments and finding people.

- **9:00 – 9:30 p.m.** Return to the apartment and plan the next day's activities.
- **10:30 p.m.** Go to bed.

Mondays we would have half the day to do laundry, shopping for the week, write emails and letters home, clean the apartment, and any wholesome approved activities if we had time to fit them in. We would also have weekly meetings in our district and zone conferences about every three months. In the mission several companionships in one area are formed into a district where one missionary is called as a district leader. Several districts in about the same region are formed into a zone where two missionaries are called as zone leaders. After that there are two missionaries called as Assistants to the missionary president. They lead the zone leaders among other things.

Missionaries have to report their efforts in each area they serve. This is done through keeping track of several different aspects of their calling each week. Examples of records kept are people contacted, lessons taught, referrals received, investigators attending church and the ultimate number of people baptized. Finding someone who is willing and ready to listen and be committed enough to become a member of the church through baptism is the ultimate goal for missionaries. It is the motivation behind all other efforts. It is essentially why they are out there, but sometimes missionaries can be so caught up in reporting good numbers and increasing the number of baptisms that they forget that the numbers represent people. The numbers a missionary companion reports are not completely indicative of all of their efforts and therefore shouldn't be the only way a missionary should feel validated. Unfortunately, since it is easy to compare numbers and not efforts many missionaries fall into the trap of only finding success through them. It is still important to have numbers so that missionary companionships can make goals to improve their efforts.

On the other hand, one problem missionaries can have, is that they focus too much on the people. Each area a companionship serves can be as small as several blocks in a city to as big as several towns. That means often only two missionaries are responsible for finding and teaching people who are ready in a pool of up to several thousand people. A hard thing is to find people who are comfortable and friendly but not showing enough interest in the message to make commitments. When this happens, the missionaries need to make the hard decision to move on to finding and teaching other people. They will leave information behind for other missionaries to come back sometime to see if these investigators are ready at another time.

JUNIORITY

It was early on that I noticed that among several groups of missionaries there was an idea spread about that you could do and teach whatever you wanted as long as you reported good numbers and convinced people to be baptized every month.

More often than not, after being trained, a missionary then becomes a junior companion to another missionary. It does not mean that they are any less important but that the senior companion usually takes on more responsibility and leads the companionship.

My first experience as junior companion was with a missionary that hardly spoke any English. He also seemed to hate me and often seemed embarrassed to be out in public with me. At the time I had only been in Argentina six weeks and was still far from being fluent in the native language. He would criticize everything I did and my language abilities nearly every time I spoke. It eventually got to the point where I didn't want to speak because I could feel a criticism coming. In a way I should've been grateful that in his own was he was trying to help me, but the way he would correct me always felt more like an attack than an act of kindness. Throughout my time as a mission I would have feelings of resentment for him and hate that I let it get to me so much. The mention of his name would bring back painful feelings. It was not until nearly the end of my mission that I would finally be able to completely forgive him. I also eventually learned that before me he had an American companion who hated being a missionary as he was only there to please his family. This missionary was notorious for spending each day messing around taking nothing seriously. I was also told by other missionaries that ever since I was transferred away my companion often had nice things to say about me and held me in high regard.

My second experience as junior companion was also with an only Spanish speaking missionary and was the hardest six weeks I ever spent in the mission. This missionary cared nothing for the mission rules. He manipulated me into believing that the mission president didn't care either. In my weekly email to the mission president I would talk about how I was concerned for this missionary because he didn't want to live any of the rules, I remember asking for help but never getting any satisfactory response on the matter.

On one occasion I told my companion I didn't agree with certain things we were doing like visiting this one mid age woman member alone for lunch. He told me if I called our mission president, I would only find out that he agreed with everything my companion was doing. I never did call because I believed him, and from then on, I knew I was left alone and had no one to back me up when I tried to do what I felt was the right thing. This companion would often tell me that obedience isn't everything and that I should stop wasting my time studying the rules and regulations. The hardest part was that just before I got there, he and his last companion had baptized 11 people in

Dear God,

one month and were widely respected by other missionaries because of it. During my time there one of the families they had baptized never attended church and would never even let us visit with them. The sister we had lunch with was also one of the new converts and she seemed confused about several things pertaining to our beliefs. She thought it was okay to still drink a little wine every now and then when our belief is strictly against the consumption of alcohol.

We only had one steady investigator in this area who was a young boy about 9 years old. Our lessons with him were behind his parents' house with just the three of us. I don't even remember his parents because we had little contact with them. We never completed all the lesson material and he even told us he hadn't read any of the Book of Mormon or prayed or done anything else we invited him to do. At the end of the month it looked like we were going to be without a baptism, so my companion and our district leader decided that they needed to meet this goal in any way possible. I felt that in no way was this kid ready for such a commitment, but I felt that as junior companion I had no say in what happened, at this point I had no reason to believe that anyone in the whole mission would sympathize with me on this matter. Sure enough, they set up a last-minute interview with this kid and it felt like the shortest interview I had ever heard of. I of course wasn't in the same room during it as interviews take place between a leader missionary and the investigator. One moment they left to do the interview and the next they were out of the room, it might have been three minutes. Any ounce of respect I had for my leader was gone the moment he signed his name on the form stating that the boy was ready. I know that maybe I had high expectations for a nine-year-

13

old, but I figured he at least needed to know that what he was about to do was serious. I felt that he should've at least been able to answer the baptismal interview questions to some comprehensive degree. Those questions are:

1. Do you believe that God is our Eternal Father? Do you believe that Jesus Christ is the Son of God and the Savior and Redeemer of the world?

2. Do you believe that the Church and gospel of Jesus Christ have been restored through the Prophet Joseph Smith? Do you believe that the current Church President is a prophet of God? What does this mean to you?

3. What does it mean to you to repent? Do you feel that you have repented of your past transgressions?

4. Have you ever committed a serious crime? If so, are you now on probation or parole? Have you ever participated in an abortion? Have you ever committed a homosexual transgression?

5. You have been taught that membership in The Church of Jesus Christ of Latter-day Saints includes living gospel standards. What do you understand about the following standards? Are you willing to obey them?
    a. The law of chastity, which prohibits any sexual relationship outside the bonds of a legal marriage between one man and one woman.
    b. The law of tithing.
    c. The Word of Wisdom.

d. The Sabbath day, including partaking of the sacrament weekly and rendering service to others.

6. When you are baptized, you covenant with God that you are willing to take upon yourself the name of Christ and keep His commandments throughout your life. Are you ready to make this covenant and strive to be faithful to it?

Failure to positively answer any of these questions does not automatically disqualify anyone from being able to be baptized, though it may indicate that they need more time.

That Saturday my companion and my leader got their baptism. The next day the boy didn't even show up to church. I was transferred to a new area the day after that and though I wanted to be the one to stay and clean up the mess with a new companion, I was just glad to be out of that companionship.

After my experience with that missionary, I was more determined to be obedient to the rules. I hated how I felt when we didn't obey the rules and I didn't want to give him the satisfaction of knowing that he broke me during my time with him. I also learned that I couldn't trust my mission president or anyone to back me up. I felt alone like I could only trust myself and the spiritual influences that guided me.

MY MISSION PRESIDENT

When I first met my mission president, I knew he was called by God through the church leaders to be in his position. He was a native but spoke English very well. I was ready to accept everything he had to say because I knew that he was led by the Spirit of God as I was. At the time I had the idea that church leaders were nearly infallible because I never had any experiences where I seemed to disagree with any of their actions in their calling. In the church of Jesus Christ of Latter-day Saints, we do not believe that anyone is or has been perfect other than Jesus and we all need to continually repent and improve ourselves to be more like Christ. This means that even leaders with great amounts of authority are still capable of error.

Once I realized that my mission president was not perfect, it seemed that the flood gates opened, and I began to notice more things that I didn't particularly agree with. One thing was that I felt that we focused too much on numbers and especially on baptisms. The focus of every training meeting seemed to be on how to convince people to say yes to a baptismal date in the first lesson. While I admit that this isn't too out of line with what our mission books told us, we still never seemed to focus on how to better focus on our investigators and be better prepared to answer their questions. It was rare that we talked about helping people understand the Book of Mormon which an essential part of our religion is. I felt like we were trying to get people baptized without even having them read any of the Book of Mormon or know who Joseph Smith was. I felt that many things I was taught in the MTC were starting to be thrown out. I had to try to convince nearly every companion I had that we needed to put things in our lessons that we were already trained to teach in the MTC.

The problem that I saw time and time again was that people would get baptized without knowing much because missionaries left things out or went through lessons too quickly without making sure people understood. It seemed like there was an idea to do whatever to get people baptized and then let them figure things out on their own. While I agree that people shouldn't take too much time hesitating with decisions, going through the process of repentance and baptism should not be taken lightly. It is supposed to be a commitment and a life changing process, and it really is only the first step toward many more commitments and processes in the future as a member of the church. I never wanted investigators to feel coerced into this decision I wanted to help them understand why they should make this commitment and then let them make the decision for themselves. Unfortunately, I saw that other missionaries just wanted their numbers and then let the local member congregations in branches or wards take over. Missionaries are supposed to work with local members to fellowship investigators and new members, but in each of my areas we had very few members attending and even fewer who had time to help. This meant that many of these new members would stop attending church all together within a month. More often than not missionaries never had follow-up lessons after baptisms either because those didn't seem lead to any desirable numbers and were seen as a waste of time. Once they got their prize baptism number, they would just leave these newly baptized members alone again.

In our mission handbook it stated that we should not visit or accept rides from individuals of the opposite sex unless another responsible adult of our own sex was also present. It told us to always obey this rule, even if the situations seem harmless. I never understood why this was up to debate and why I never received a straight answer whenever I brought this up. My mission president on several occasions told me that some missions interpreted it to be different things, but never told me what our mission interpretation was. I was left to try and follow it to my best ability. The problem was that most of the people who would listen to us were women without men in the home, and we didn't have many active male members who were able to come with us. Every time my companionship changed, I had to bring this up and try my best to convince the other missionaries of what I believed, all while knowing that I had no back up from most other missionaries including my leaders and the president. No one ever gave me a clear answer. Some said that "you should just follow the spirit", or that "it's ok if you're outside, or if she has children at home", or I was even told, "that doesn't really apply to South America". Though I never felt good about what we were doing and tried often to avoid the situation, I admit that many times I just went along with it when we would swap companions with others for a day with missionaries that just ignored the rule. This made it harder to trust my mission president as once again he left us all to figure it out on our own.

Dear God,

I soon learned that my mission president's hands-off approach was partly due to the strictness of the mission president before him. Apparently, the previous president was so strict that it incited a group of missionaries to form a rebellious group. Throughout my mission service I heard many rumors of how this group was started and how bad they were. The subject came up often as many of those missionaries had previously served in most of the areas where I served. There were stories ranging from a tv and x-box being passed around to one of the main leaders being an adulterer and mixed up in drugs. I was told that most of those missionaries had returned home and the group was disbanded by the time I arrived.

THE NEW FEELING

My next companion was American and only had three months left in his two-year term. After some adjustments we were able to find success in a difficult area. My time with him revitalized my hope in doing things the right way. He would agree with me on many things. Right before it was time for him to return home, we baptized a young man who was in no doubt ready for the commitment. This companion left soon afterward and though I was sad to see him go I could tell that he ended his mission on a good note.

After him I would finally be promoted to senior companion. Though I now had more responsibilities and a little more say in how my companionships would work, I still faced an uphill battle as I had to once again teach my companions the importance of following rules and convince them to follow me. Some of them would actually agree with me, but others would reluctantly follow me. My first junior companion fell under this category and I learned that he complained often about me to my mission president. I still worked hard, and we had more success in that area before I left. We helped a family return to the church and the father was able to baptize his children the day after I was transferred.

In my next area I would eventually convince another two companions to work with me and we would

Dear God,

have some success. It was about two months in this area that I started to notice things a little differently. I woke up one morning with an eerie feeling that something was coming to an end. I wasn't sure if it meant that the end of my mission was near, the end of my life, or even the end of the world. I still continued to exercise, study, and prepare just like any other day. While we went about our plans, I soon began feeling stronger and stronger that it was going to be my last day. I still had no idea as to whether or not it meant that I would die or be released as a missionary. As the day went by, I was never faced with anything life threatening or that could possibly merit my dismissal as a missionary. When we returned to the apartment after working, I was sure that during that night I would either pass away in my sleep or something catastrophic would happen. I prepared for each possibility. I made sure I told my companion that I appreciated him, and I even left a note for him essentially telling him everything he needed to know about the locals since he was still somewhat new to the area. I also wrote to send them my love. When I awoke the next morning, I was troubled and confused to still be there. Nothing happened. I quickly took the note and hid it before my companion woke up. The feeling still stayed with me throughout the day, but once again nothing happened that day and after preparing again that night, I awoke the next morning confused.

  This would continue every day for about the next 3 months. Every day was my last day, and every morning I awoke to disappointment and confusion. I began to wonder if despite all my efforts to have a perfect last day maybe I still wasn't doing something right.

  During this time, I noticed that I also began to feel

21

the Spirit's influence just a little differently. It seemed to influence me to do more trivial things; wear a certain tie, walk a certain path. There were many times I felt to knock on doors that were never answered. Unfortunately, these trivial things never seemed to lead to anything. It is not completely uncommon for missionaries to go through this as it may be a way for God to test their obedience, but my tests seemed to be more frequent and became more extreme. I once approached a ferocious pitbull in the rain, so I could ring a bell behind him that no one answered. Luckily it was chained up but if I had made any wrong steps it would've been able to attack me.

Even though a lot of these experiences led to nothing, I did still have good experiences and inspired moments. I was soon made to be district leader of the missionaries in the two small towns where I was. There was only one other companionship other than mine. On one occasion while doing morning study I felt that my companion and I should go over to the other town and have an immediate exchange. We left right away and showed up at the other missionaries' apartment unannounced. I was sure something bad was happening there so when we knocked, I was ready for anything. After a few minutes they finally answered, but everything seemed fine. We still went about the day working in that area, and at the end of the day nothing had happened. This incident may or may not have been connected to another where again I felt to go over, but only this time it was at the end of the day. We were with a member having a lesson with his ex-wife who wasn't a member. As soon as I felt the prompting to leave, I prayed that if it was really something we should do that God would provide a way for us to get over to the other town, since at this time the busses were off for the night and we didn't have a car. Right after the lesson I asked our member if he would take us over and he did. That night my companion and one of the other missionaries came back to our area and I stayed in the other town. While there I discovered text messages on their phone, which was against missionary rules. I didn't say anything at the time but just copied them and sent them to our phone. We went about the day working, and nothing else of much note happened that day.

About a week later one of my zone leaders came to visit and I brought up the incident, we called the number and found out that on one day during companionship exchanges when my companion and the senior companion were working in our area, they visited a family of members all of which were women. They told us that at one point this other missionary was outside with the younger woman while my companion was inside. Apparently, they flirted, exchanged numbers, and had been texting ever since. The member ladies told us that they didn't like how he was acting around her but didn't know how to say anything. On the day I had our second emergency visit, the two other missionaries were invited to go over and have lunch with these ladies which was another rule they were going to break. When my leader and I got to the bottom of it all, he told me he would inform our mission president. I never learned more of the situation.

One thing I did learn though was that the junior companion was dealing with depression along with several other problems and desperately wanted to go home. My mission president did everything he could to convince him to stay. I was even told by his companion that he was given freedom to do anything he could to make sure this missionary didn't go home. From his demeanor in explaining this to me, he seemed to be under the impression that they were exempt from all rules. If they wanted to work one day then that was fine, and if not then they could just take the day off. I have no doubt that this is what lead to the inappropriate relationship I had discovered. Once again, I did not agree with my mission president just like several occasions before but was unsure if I had the right to ask questions and tell him how I really felt. I still don't understand why he didn't inform me of this conversation he had with this companionship telling them to practically throw out their responsibility to God. For all I knew they were lying to me, but at the time it didn't seem to me like it was beyond him.

On one of my last days in that area as I was doing the trivial things, I was now more accustomed to, I began to feel like each task lead me closer to the end I was now hoping for. It almost seemed like a game I was playing with God as each task somehow led to another seemingly insignificant yet somehow purposeful event that I knew would eventually end it all. After completing several tasks and at a moment where we were very pressed for time to get to an appointment, we had already set up to teach I felt to knock on a door. As I approached the door, I envisioned myself collapsing and waking up in a hospital with my family all around me. The happy experience was so close I could taste it, but I hesitated and quickly the feeling left me. I could no longer feel the spiritual influence I lived for. I didn't knock on the door right away and I felt that in my hesitation I had sinned against God. I was now being punished and could no longer feel any influence at all. I had no guidance as to what to teach in our lesson as we hadn't come prepared, but I remember talking about

Dear God,

sinning and losing the influence of God. I was now unsure of everything, but we still continued forward with our scheduled plans. The whole time I was silently pleading with God to forgive me. I was beginning to wonder if I had ruined everything, I had come to hope for in being released from this painful state of mind. By the end of the day I was devastated and could feel God's frustration as now he must have had to change His plans for me because of my hesitation. Why couldn't I have just knocked?

Once again, the next day began with the impending end drawing closer, and once again it never came. I soon came to accept this more as just a lingering thought than an imminent danger. I guess I had come to terms with it. I would still act as though every day was my last, but I stopped being so hopeful. If it came, I would welcome it and if not, then I would just continue working. It was fairly soon after that I was transferred to my next area.

THE "REVELATION"

The day I traveled to my new area I met a young woman on the bus who seemed fairly receptive to me and what I had to say. By the time we arrived I already had her contact information with a good time frame of when to meet her and her family to share our message. When I met my new companion, I was finally revitalized and ready to go. From the start we got along pretty well since he was very new to the mission and mostly unscathed by the influence of other missionaries. We worked hard for several weeks and even had a baptism. During this whole time, I hadn't had many trivial promptings though the eerie feeling of the end approaching everyday was still in the back of my mind.

One feeling that I had when I first met the local church leaders was that the Bishop was not a trustworthy person. I had no reason why I felt that way in particular, but I just did. Throughout my time there we didn't do much to work with him.

I soon began to feel this darkness around me and especially in a certain part of town that we eventually began to avoid. It seemed to follow me, but nothing ever happened.

One day my companion and I visited some local

Dear God,

members and were surprised to meet a friend of one of them that had questions about the church. I do not recall her name, but as we began to teach her, I began to feel that she was somehow connected with me. We continued through each lesson. While teaching I began to feel as though my spirit was in another realm, and somehow, she was there with me. In my mind I could see her being baptized, but for some reason it had to be right away. It had to be that night. As we continued through each lesson, I began to have a vision of us going to the church and everything being prepared for the baptism. My mission president would even be there to interview her and authorize the ordinance. The only thing was that I needed to teach her everything and get her to agree to go through with it. When we finally brought up baptism, the spiritual feeling left me, so I didn't have the courage to bring up what I was thinking. Before we left, I said a long prayer with them. I prayed trying to influence her to ask to be baptized but not using those words exactly.

Afterward the prayer I tried to linger a bit and even asked her if she wanted to ask us anything more, but after a moment of silence I gave up and we began to leave. On our way back to the apartment I felt that we should go back. I felt that she just needed a little time and then she would have the courage to ask. I convinced my companion to come with me without telling him exactly why and we headed back. Upon approaching the door, the Spirit once again left me, so we headed back. A few yards away I once again felt to go back so I began to go back but this time she was just leaving with another man and they offered to give us a ride home since it was late. The spiritual feeling returned, and I knew this was the opportunity. I felt that all we needed to do was get her to the church, so I asked her

27

friend to drop us off there. On the way I felt that we needed to stop and talk to someone on the street, but I just didn't have the courage to ask them to stop. Once we finally made it to the church the lights were off, and no one was there. As I got out of the car I asked once more if she had any more questions, hoping that she now had the courage to ask to be baptized. She said once again that she didn't, and they dropped us off. Once again, I failed. I knew that it was because since we didn't stop and talk to the person on the street. They were the key. Somehow talking to them would've set off a series of events that would've led to the whole vision I had earlier coming true.

It was very late for missionaries to be out, but we just sat there in front of the church until my companion finally asked me what was going on. I told him I didn't know why I felt to be there. I felt spiritually compelled not to tell him the truth. He suggested we leave, and I eventually gave in. As we left, I felt again to go back, but this time after a couple steps back my companion stopped me and reminded me how late it was. I didn't want to give up, I didn't want the spiritual feeling to leave again but I didn't have any clear answers, so I listened, and we walked back to our apartment.

The next day I was broken. I lacked any direction or confidence. Once again, I also had no hope in finally being released. I didn't listen to the spiritual influence and so if left me. Every so often our apartments get inspected to make sure that we have adequate living conditions and that everything is clean a working well. That morning we had our apartment inspected and were told to do some deep cleaning. I prided myself for how well I kept things clean throughout the mission, but I hadn't had sufficient time to do a deep cleaning since I first came to the area. We went straight to the store and bought supplies. Once we returned, we began cleaning everything. Apparently, I was very caught up into it because soon it was night and my companion went to bed. I felt that I had to get the cleaning done that night. As I frantically cleaned, I noticed some dark residue over all the appliances and especially the stove and oven. I soon discovered dirty baking pans covered in grease shoved under it. While I began cleaning them, I felt as though I was cleaning away a different kind of darkness. I soon learned from the spiritual influence that the reason for the urgency was because God was going to come to our apartment. This made me clean even harder trying to find and get rid of every tiny speck of the residue. As I continued cleaning, I had another revelation. The dark residue and greasy pans were from a burnt offering that the group of rebellious missionaries from before my time made to curse the missionary work in the land. That night I also periodically felt to tell my companion that God was coming so I did. I ended up waking him up and telling him three times, but each time he fell back asleep. Eventually I was somewhat satisfied with my cleaning and went to bed figuring that maybe God wasn't coming that night but soon.

I woke up that next morning and began personal scripture study as normal. This time I decided to read the Book of Mormon from the beginning. I soon felt compelled to read out loud. I read the first 8 chapters but soon I began reading it all backwards. Then all of a sudden, I began to replace words in verses with my own. It was as though I was being shown that a change to everything was soon about to happen. In the first several chapters of the Book of Mormon there is a story about a man named Nephi who is sent by his father, a prophet, to get a record from a wicked man. Nephi comes upon this man who is drunk, and he is spiritually prompted to kill him in order to get the record. Nephi hesitates because it is a commandment from God that man should not kill, but the prompting persists, and he is told that for God's purposes it is ok and even according to the laws of the time since the man stole the records his death was justified. I knew that reading this account at that time wasn't just coincidence and it must have had some significant meaning.

God must have been telling me that I needed to do something that pushed the boundaries of his commandments for the greater good. Luckily, I never felt that it meant I needed to kill anyone. I had remembered the whole ordeal the night before with the investigator and how I felt spiritually connected to her. I also thought about the burnt residue. Soon I felt that the two incidents were connected. She must have been there when the offering was burnt. I felt that the group of rebellious missionaries must have engaged in sexual intercourse with her as part of the offering to curse the land. I pieced it together that in order to reverse the curse I needed to make a pure offering to God. Since I was a virgin, as part of the offering I needed to give up that part of myself with her. It would be pure because I didn't want it and had been saving that part of myself for my future wife. God must have been coming to accept the offering.

I did question the whole reasoning at first but decided that if I had already gone this far, I might as well see it through to the end. I figured that such an act that would impact the whole mission would need to be approved at least by at least the General Authority that was a leader

Dear God,

over my mission president if not by the Prophet himself. I knew that in order for it to get that far I needed to work up the chain of command as we were told to do so instead of directly going to higher leaders. I was the district leader, so I first contacted my zone leaders and told them about what I was feeling. I'm not sure if my explanation was complete enough or if they understood what I was saying but somehow one of them told me that if I really felt like God was telling me to do it I should go ahead and do it. I made it through the first check point and later that night I called the assistants to the mission president. I do not remember much of what they said but they discouraged me, so they must have understood more than my other leaders. The next day my Mission President called but apparently my explanation of things was very hard to understand and so he decided to visit us. At the time he showed up, I was cleaning and preparing for God to come. I was also receiving another revelation. I began organizing my clothes in a certain way. I hung up three white shirts then my black pants and then another white shirt I didn't know the significance, but I knew I would find out soon. Once he finally got my attention, he tried to ask me a few questions. I knew that my companion had to be the one to tell him first in order for him to believe so I excused myself to the bathroom. I waited until my companion finished telling him all the things I had been doing and saying the past couple of days and then I finally came out.

I first began to tell him all the things I didn't agree with about how he was running things that I had kept bottled up inside and about how important rules were. I then told him everything else that was on my mind. He stopped me and then suggested that I might be OCD. He then read to us some scripture I didn't pay attention to and then said,

31

"you feel that Elders? That is the Spirit". At that point I felt nothing. I neither felt the newer spiritual feeling I gained on the mission nor any other older spiritual feelings I had in the past. It was that moment that awoke me to the idea that maybe something was seriously wrong. Either I had been following evil spirits or there was something wrong with my mind. I was completely lost, I had a million questions now and wasn't sure how to get the answers. If the very spiritual influence I had felt for nearly a year and a half now that was with me when I taught about God and His plan for us, and gave me purpose in life didn't come from the Spirit of God then what was it? I was blank.

My president seemed satisfied with his OCD diagnosis and confident that I just needed to get back to work. He soon left us there to it and I admit I was almost about to trust his judgment. I resolved that it was best to just get back to work. However, when I decided to work the next day we were in the middle of a lesson and I was teaching about how God wants us to make our own decisions. I realized right then that with the confusion I was going through maybe I never had a choice myself whether or not to believe. Maybe my decisions were solely based on what other people wanted. Everything was foggy, and I don't remember how much time I spent analyzing everything. At one point I questioned whether or not my companion even existed. I wasn't sure if anything was real. The thought came to me that maybe this whole life was just a dream because somehow things connected too well. I figured maybe I needed to wake up and that the only way I could was to kill myself. There was a knife on the counter, and I could see myself putting it inside my chest. It wouldn't hurt because I couldn't feel anything in this moment. I envisioned stabbing myself like a balloon and popping myself awake.

Dear God,

Before actually acting on that thought I figured maybe I should say a prayer. I dropped to my knees and began praying, "Dear God, if there is a God and this is not all just in my mind, please help me know what is real". I got up and sat down on the small couch in our apartment and thought for a moment. I tried to remember anything from my past that would give me any amount of clarity. The only thought I could remember was when I was in Nauvoo and how peaceful it was. I remembered the moments where I felt that Joseph Smith was actually a prophet and the moment when I first finished reading the Book of Mormon. I realized that everything else was unclear, but I could not deny those moments and the peaceful spiritual feelings they had stirred inside me.

Though I at least had those moments to rely on I still didn't know what else was real and I knew I could no longer teach. I needed to find answers before I could teach anyone anything ever again. I decided that maybe if I took a little time, I could probably figure out what was happening and why I was "OCD" as if it was a problem I could figure out and fix. I never thought that maybe I was going through something that couldn't be fixed. I began to analyze my life and see how this condition could've developed. There had to be a reason why I was this way. There had to be a solution. There had to be a way to go back to being myself again.

MY PLEA FOR CLARITY

After taking some time to reflect on my life I was able to actually notice a pattern of misjudgment. Before the mission I would often start to like someone but then quickly become obsessed with them. Many times, I had confessed feelings of love to women with whom I only shared a handful of conversations. I figured that subconsciously I must have known that I was ruining whatever potential I might have had with them by being so clingy. I then realized that in a way by rushing things and subconsciously pushing them away I was being abusive. This is where I figured that I must have learned somewhere that abuse and feelings of love and desire were connected. I traced the pattern of times I had sabotaged things and major events in my life until it finally seemed to stop at one awful incident.

When I was just about six, I remembered an experience of sexual experimentation. I could not remember a lot of details but that there were a couple of girl cousins and another boy cousin. We played a game where the girl cousins would take off their clothes and we would hug. This experience had always baffled me because all of us cousins were about the same age. Seeing as I couldn't seem

Dear God,

to remember or figure out who the ring leader was or who actually suggested the game, I concluded that it really could've been me. But how at such a young age could I know about such things? Where did I learn such an idea for a game? For the life of me I couldn't remember anything of such note that happened before this time. I could not remember being exposed to anything pornographic or sexual at this age as pornography is shunned by our religion. My mind raced to the idea that maybe there was an experience so awful of the same nature earlier that it was blocked out of my mind.

Not long before the time of these experimental games, my family had moved away from some of my other relatives. I thought hard and tried to focus on anything of note that could've happened. I did vaguely remember an experience where I was with one of my girl cousins in an old camper trailer outside of my grandparent's house. I remembered a big bed with a red quilt on it and that one of my uncles was living with my grandparents at the time. I quickly pieced this together with a two other experiences to try and figure out an answer.

The first experience was a nightmare I had once that scared me deeply as a kid where I saw my uncle appear outside my bedroom window with a blue hue in his skin. The second experience happened just months before becoming a missionary. I was home alone and for some reason needed to find something at night in an old camper we had out behind the house. I remembered opening the door and being so frightened I slammed it, got into our car, and drove around for a while before I could recompose myself. Putting all this together I came to the conclusion that I must have had a sexually disturbing experience with my

35

uncle and cousin. I was OCD and following pseudo-spirits because for some reason my mind was trying to get me to remember this awful experience, so I could finally come to terms with it. I felt at that time I really needed to speak to a psychiatrist or someone that could help me further confront this incident and help me figure out who I really was. The problem was that with devoting my time 24/7 to finding people and teaching them, I knew there was no way I was going to be able to focus on the mission and myself. I also greatly feared that this was the only time my mind would be able to open up like this. I knew that if I just forgot about it all and got to work like I was told several times, I might go back into denial about it all. I needed time to process it all. I desperately wanted to be admitted to a psychiatric ward. I figured maybe I could be hypnotized to remember the experience better and confront it. I decided to call my mission president and ask to see him. He didn't seem overly thrilled to hear from me again after I'm sure he thought he had already solved my problems.

    The morning my companion and I went to see him I had to wait almost 2 hours beyond our scheduled time and I took it as though he was telling me that I was wasting his time. When he finally arrived, he first talked to me alone in his office. I told him everything that I had figured and left nothing back. Then I told him that I needed to see a psychiatrist or someone as soon as possible. I told him that I needed someone who spoke English and I needed to see them in person, so I could be comfortable enough to have them help me work things out. I suggested this meant that more than likely I needed to either go home for a while to just focus on it or I needed to be admitted somewhere where I could find help. All things considered I told him that it probably wasn't best for me to still be a full time missionary. He didn't like the idea of sending me home but agreed that I should take a little time to figure some things out and speak to someone and see what happens.

After our conversation, he met with my companion alone then with both of us together and told us that we should go back and continue working. He then said that in about a day a psychiatrist would call me since the only one they had available was based out of Buenos Aires. I was mad that he still didn't seem to take it all seriously. I opened up my whole soul to him and told him how I felt I needed to be helped but he didn't listen. I decided not to cause a scene and my companion, and I left back to our area. On our way back, I began to feel that if I took my mind off of everything that had happened and got back to work, I would just slip back into denial. That meant maybe I'd never have another chance to know what happened or know who I was. Going back to work was not an option. Even if I wanted to how could I when I didn't know anything for sure anymore? I wasn't sure what the Spirit actually felt like so how was I supposed to follow it? And how was I supposed to teach others to follow it?

I remember looking in the mirror that night and noticing confusion all throughout my body. My eyes were brown but up close they always had a bit of green. Did this mean I was really meant to have green eyes instead? My hair always had a mixture of blonde and brown, and yet in pictures I remember my hair was bleach blonde when I was about the age of the incident in question. Was my hair really supposed to be blonde after all? In school I was often told I wrote weird like a left-handed person when I was always right handed. Also, at a younger age it was sometimes difficult for me to remember which hand was which. Did this actually mean I was supposed to be left handed? Had this experience been so traumatic that it robbed my body of knowing what it really was?

After being indoors all day trying to focus and remember everything, the psychologist finally called. I don't remember a lot about what she said but the tone I got from her seemed to say I was wasting her time and making a big deal out of nothing. She told me that forgetting myself and getting back to work was what I needed because I was on God's time and then after I finish the next 6 months, I could think about me. I opened up my soul to another person who let me down and didn't seem to get how important this was. I could hardly wait another day without answers how could I ever go six months? I later called my mission president and told him that it wasn't working out for me, that I needed to see professional help in person and that I really felt that I should go home. He told me again that I should just get back to work and tried to make me feel guilty saying that if I just came home for something like this that it wouldn't look good for him. I told him I made up my mind and that if I had to get home on my own somehow, I would. He finally gave in but said I couldn't just go home right away, and that it would take time to process things. I told him I would wait awhile but I needed to get back as soon as possible. He allowed me to talk to my parents and tell them everything that was going on.

I went to a nearby phone Kiosk and called. Once they picked up, I felt somewhat relieved to hear their voices. I soon explained everything yet another time without holding back. I told them I needed to get home and talk to my cousin about the experience in mind. The Uncle in question had already passed away years ago so she was the only source I had to finding out what really happened. I asked my mom what I was like when I was younger. I pointed out that I noticed that when I was younger, I thought I was more outgoing and fearless but soon after I became the silent less confident type. I don't remember what else was said but I remember that I wasn't completely satisfied with the conversation. Just after hanging up the phone in anger, my right foot curved inward and for a little while I couldn't walk with it straight. I was born pigeon-toed and I figured that my body was reverting back to the incident in question. This was a definite sign that I was following the right lead. This only further fired my determination that I needed to keep these thoughts and feelings fresh and not slip back into denial.

The next day my mission president called and made several different proposals to keep me in the mission until my release date. One idea was that I could keep my current leadership title but that privately my companion would do all the work. Another was that I could work in the office and do whatever I felt up to doing. I was not at all tempted by any of these ideas, as I already witnessed a missionary in this condition. I didn't feel like I wanted to waste any more time. I despised missionaries who sat around and did nothing. Once again, I told him that I needed to go home and that I would go find my own way if I had to. I didn't care about whether or not I was honorably released at the time, I just needed to go home.

The next couple of days I was miserable. I had told everyone that my companion could go out and work with locals while I stayed in the apartment because I was no longer working. They didn't trust me to be by myself, so another companionship came to work. Though I hated and fought this decision at the time, I'm now glad that they had the sense to not listen to me and go through with this plan. At one point I wanted to just find a building and jump off of it. I even contemplated strangling myself with one of my ties. I wanted all of these problems finally gone. Somewhere somehow, I still had a tiny speck of hope that maybe if I finally got a chance to confront this haunting memory it would all go away.

While the other companionship was there one of the missionaries would babysit me and the other was supposed to work with my companion. My companion and the other missionary ended up staying inside with us most of the time. I remember being super frustrated one day that they were not doing any work. It must have seemed so hypocritical that I confronted them on this but clearly, I was not in my right state of mind and supposedly they were. I nearly punched one of them in the face when he started talking back to me. At times I wished I had hit him, but the fact that I was still able to hold back meant that I wasn't completely out of touch with reality.

From the time I had my last phone call with my president to the time I finally was able to come home must have been about a week, but it felt much longer. I didn't expect it to take that long. If I had cancer or some other urgent physical illness they wouldn't have waited that long for sure, but in all fairness we all had limited information about what was going on. I was finally told I could go home and was sent my itinerary for my flight that following Monday. Unfortunately, this meant that I had to endure one last Sunday. I desperately did not want to go to church, but the other elders insisted. The stress of it all caused me to have a severe headache which was only eased by putting my hand on the side of my face. It became so tense that I couldn't move my hand at all. Soon I put my other hand against my other temple to ease the painful tingling sensation, but it glued as well. I could not move either of my hands from my head and had to walk into church with both hands covering my face. It would be hours before I could move them. In the middle of Sacrament meeting I started crying and left to the bathroom. I was so embarrassed I locked myself in a stall. The Bishop soon came in and convinced me to visit with him in his office. As we talked, I began to see he wasn't the man I thought I was working with all these weeks. He was actually a good man and actually comforted me.

The next day I finally headed to the mission office and got my tickets. My mission president didn't show up to see me off or tell me anything at all. The office elders gave me the ticket and took me to the airport. The last thing they said to me was, "go home, fix whatever it is you need to fix, and then come back".

MY NOT SO TRIUMPHANT RETURN

Being the youngest of five returned missionaries, I always had an idea of what it would be like coming home. I often thought about it and envisioned how surreal it would be. I could see my family anxiously waiting to see me. I could see smiles on their faces while holding a welcome home poster. I could see my cousins there too and everyone waiting to give me a hug and talk about how much I've changed. It would be an amazing surreal moment.

When I came home I never had any of that. I told my family that I just wanted to be checked into a mental facility right away. I couldn't handle any resemblance of the happy moment I had wanted before. So instead of smiles and anxious excitement I got confused looks and awkward moments. In no way do I blame them for their reactions. It was a very confusing time, and honestly, I was led to believe that despite being honorably released I was turning my back on God. My relapse only further enforced these feelings. I didn't deserve any happy reception from anyone. I felt that for sure if they knew I had given in to my old addiction that there wouldn't have been anything honorable about my release. Everyone in the mission must have thought the worse about me for leaving so early. The missionaries I was with at the end treated me like I was just giving up. Surely by now they spread the word, and everyone must have seen me as the coward I now saw in myself. I didn't expect anything different from my family.

Though I knew I didn't deserve it, I just wanted to get started right away working with professional help, so I could finally get some clarity. I was not afraid of facing the dreadful experience with my uncle, I just wanted to get it over with.

I had figured that I would be okay with just talking to a therapist, but my parents insisted I see a psychiatrist as well. I first saw the therapist and began talking about the experience in mind and how I could find a way to confront it. I never told him about the experiences that led to this belief, because he didn't seem very interested in those details. Though we did address my relapse, he didn't seem to understand where I was coming from or what I needed. We mostly laid out plans for our future visits and though I still didn't have any answers I felt like I had at least made some progress.

When I finally went to the psychiatrist, I didn't think it was necessary and had no idea what he could do to help me. He insisted that I tell him why I felt that I was repressing a memory and what events lead to this belief. Immediately after I told him a few things about following a belief that I needed to break a curse through making an offering to God he stopped me and told me that all of that was a text-book case of a manic episode. He further explained that this meant that I was Bipolar and would need meds to control my mood swings and prevent severe episodes like this in the future. He also told me that given this condition it would not be recommended for me to return as a missionary. My repressed memory wasn't real. My mission was over.

As I went through all the confusion of coming home I never thought that I would NEVER be able to go back. My plan was to fix myself and then return and finish the rest of the six months I had left of my two-year term. I figured at the very least I would eventually be reassigned to another mission within the United States as is common for American missionaries who have gone abroad and returned home to recover from illness. It was hard for me to accept this news.

My parents live in a small town where everyone knows everyone, and everyone's business is public record. When I came home, I wasn't sure how I would be received by the town. I just knew that from the surface I was the guy who returned early and didn't seem to show signs of any serious medical conditions. I figured that if anyone was paying attention, they most likely came to the conclusion that I came home because of depression as it was something that wasn't completely rare at the time. I never knew who was actually paying attention but assumed that everyone probably had already made up their mind about me. I wouldn't blame them if they thought the worst of me, in fact I would've empathized with them more than anyone who gave me the benefit of the doubt.

Several times my brother would take me with him to play basketball with other locals at the school. Though I hadn't shot a basket in over a year and was never very good to begin with, I was somewhat glad to be out. I finally didn't have to talk to interact all I had to do was play. We played several different games and switched up teams. Each game didn't mean anything in the long run, and I didn't realize how much I needed to do something that didn't matter. Many of the other players were actually members of the church and several had served missions. I never knew if word ever got around to them about my situation at the time, but I did know that they didn't treat me any different than a guy who's only redeeming quality was that he was tall enough to get rebounds.

In a way I did wish that everyone knew what was going on with me. If only they knew the confusing hell I had just endured. If only they knew how I had to fight to come home, how my mind warped the spiritual important things to me, or how I nearly killed myself just weeks before. I wished they understood the seriousness of my condition because I felt so alone. I wanted someone to be there with me to just reassure me that I wasn't completely hopeless, but I knew that even if I could explain everything they still wouldn't understand. I hardly understood it all and I experienced it firsthand.

I spent a lot of time running when I lived at home. Long distance running was hard for me growing up and I had always hated it. I never would've thought that one day it would be one of my only sources of solace. Since I had spent the last 18 months mostly walking everywhere in my areas and doing cardio exercises 20 minutes a day six days a week I was in pretty good shape. For once I had the stamina to run longer than I could ever go before. When I finally felt like I couldn't go further I pushed myself until I couldn't feel anything. In a way it was like I was able to feel accomplished and beat myself up all at the same time. I felt like I deserved to be punished but each run would never be enough. Maybe I really should've listened to my leader. Maybe I could've stayed in the mission and served out the rest of my time. Like many times before, I sabotaged another potentially good thing in my life.

It is customary in the church for honorably released and returned missionaries to give a talk in front of the church congregation soon after their return. I was quick to start working with my Bishop about my repentance process for a relapse I had during all the confusion, but I soon found it too hard to abstain. Because of my continual addictive behavior at the time I was no longer found in good standing in the church and I would never get a chance to give that talk. Even though I was now unworthy to participate in several things, I still attended church because I didn't want to turn my back on God completely. Though I was still confused about many things, I still knew that I felt better about life when I was actively going to church. I soon began to recognize the familiar feelings of peace and hope that I felt many times before the mission and the times during it when I wasn't confused with the other "spiritual" feelings.

HEALING

Though we have made many advancements in our understanding of mental illness in our society, it still seems to be widely misunderstood by the general population. Along with this misunderstanding comes with the false notions about being on medication for said illnesses. Whenever we speak of someone who has mental problems and on meds it is rarely a good light we're shedding on them. That is why it takes courage to first accept your diagnosis and then accept that medication can help.

When I came home, I was miserable and had bad mood swings. I also was still hungry for answers and determined to find a way back to my old self. I missed the old me. I missed being able to care about other people and other things beyond myself. Somehow, I still thought it was possible to get back and though my diagnosis was not what I expected to be dealing with, I was at least willing to give meds a try. I figured that they at least couldn't make my life any worse or more confusing than it was already.

It took a while before I notice much of a change as I took my medication. It also took a while before my psychiatrist and I could find the right combination and dosage of meds for me to finally feel stable again. It was a slow transition and didn't happen overnight, but slowly I did start to feel less agitated. I was also able to have more control over my energy levels. I was finally able to regularly sleep through the night. Though the meds have helped me a lot to live a somewhat normal life, they haven't cured my mental illness. There is no cure for being Bipolar it is a life sentence and though I haven't had any major manic episodes, suicidal thoughts, or severe mood swings since my mission it is still something I have to accept and deal with everyday I take my pills.

Early on I was taught by my psychiatrist to think of my medication like it was for high blood pressure. If I had high blood pressure and didn't take my medication, then I would be setting myself up for the possibility of a heart attack. If I don't take my medication, then I'm setting myself up for the possibility of another extreme manic episode. During my last episode I nearly died so there's no telling what I would be led to believe or even if I would survive another episode like it.

My life today is in no way perfect, but I know that I owe a lot of its stability to the regime I'm on. I never have completely returned to the old me, and the truth is I never will. After an experience like the one I had, how could I ever go back to being the same person I was before? I can say however that I have since been able to process things a lot better now and that I now have a much better grip on reality. I am not saying that meds will fix all problems or that everyone should be on them. I just know they have helped me.

Because of my new-found stability I eventually began to realize a few things about my whole mission experience that I may never have come to understand otherwise. I came to see through all the confusing moments even from the beginning I still had moments I know were inspired. While in the MTC I submitted a friend's name to be prayed about, when I returned I learned that at about that same time she had a manic episode. I never got a lot of detail from her about the situation, but I know she was blessed.

I also came to realize that though I didn't agree with everything my mission president did, I may have misjudged him on several things. Instead of a controlling authority figure, I began to see that he did have good intentions at times. I never thought that maybe I was the first missionary to open up to him about everything and that he didn't know how to deal with it. I never thought that maybe he had little to no understanding of mental illnesses and couldn't see the signs that were there. I realized that like the Bishop in my last area, many of my negative feelings toward him were misguided. I was eventually able to forgive him for the way he treated me.

I also eventually came to realize that a lot of my feelings and generalizations about the other missionaries were unfair. I would see a few missionaries act a certain way and then assume that everyone was the same. Though I did witness several things I did not agree with, I began to realize that like me they were not perfect. I also realized that though I obeyed the rules strictly and tried to do everything right, I wasn't perfect either. I was finally able to understand mercy and extend it to the other missionaries. I cannot say that everything I felt or experienced throughout my whole mission was false, but I can say that somethings weren't exactly as I perceived.

It took years to finally be able to come to these realizations.

After I was finally stable and ready enough, with the

help of my oldest brother I was able to move out and into an apartment in a big city nearby. At the time I was still struggling with abstinence and addiction recovery, but I still attended church and became active with meeting other young single adults like me. I was eventually able to abstain long enough to be in good standing again with the church. I was even given responsibilities. I was able to have a couple of relationships and several good friendships. I was fortunate to eventually find my future wife there. We were married in the temple in Gilbert, Arizona on December 12, 2014. We now have a two-year-old son and though we do not have the perfect life, we are active members of the church and happy.

Made in United States
Orlando, FL
17 June 2023